George Fisk Comfort

The Land Troubles in Ireland

A historical, political and economical study

George Fisk Comfort

The Land Troubles in Ireland
A historical, political and economical study

ISBN/EAN: 9783337325794

Printed in Europe, USA, Canada, Australia, Japan

Cover: Foto ©ninafisch / pixelio.de

More available books at **www.hansebooks.com**

THE LAND TROUBLES

IN IRELAND.

———•———

A Historical, Political and Economical Study.

—BY—

PROF. G. F. COMFORT, A. M.,
OF SYRACUSE UNIVERSITY.

———•———

SYRACUSE, N. Y.:
JOHN T. ROBERTS.
1881.

The Land Troubles in Ireland.

*ARTICLE I.

GEOGRAPHICAL FEATURES OF IRELAND.

As is well known, Ireland is the most westerly body of land in Europe. It lies between North Latitude 51° 26′ and 55° 21′, being at the same distance north of the Equator as Labrador in the Western and Kamtschatka in the Eastern Hemisphere. It is the first land to catch the warm current and the moist, westerly breezes of the Gulf Stream. By this island as a breakwater, the mild current of this stream is divided into two parts, one of which moves southwards, enters the British Channel, and laves the shores of France, Belgium, Holland, Germany, Denmark and Norway, mollifying the climate of north-western Europe; the other portion passes by Scotland and on into the Arctic Ocean.

The constant current of warm air from over the Gulf Stream gives to Ireland a uniformity of temperature that is not to be found elsewhere in Europe, nor scarcely, in so large body of land, in the whole world. The general temperature in the vicinity of Dublin is about 50° Fahrenheit. The average temperature of the hottest and the coldest months rarely varies more than ten degrees from this standard. In winter the average temperature is 40°; in spring and autumn it is 50°; and in summer it is 60°. Of these limits, the lowest is not sufficiently cold to check the growth of herbage, nor the highest sufficiently intense to parch the surface of a moist soil or to scorch its luxuriant grasses. Hence the fields and lawns maintain a perpetual verdure at all seasons of the year. Lands can be sowed to grass at any time, even in December. The grazier never loses the benefit of his rich pastures, except during the passage of a

*The matter contained in these pages was incorporated in a series of newspaper articles that were printed in the *Northern Christian Advocate* during January, February and March, 1881. The author has carefully revised and considerably amplified the original text for this reprint. The publisher thought fit to retain the term " Article " to designate the divisions of the subject.

fleeting fall of snow. Cattle thus attain to a perfection which
they seldom acquire in other lands, and this with comparatively
little care and expense. With this remarkable uniformity of mild
climate the inhabitants of the Emerald Isle, which is clad in
perpetual greeness, require much less fuel than those of colder
and bleaker climates. Less variety of clothing also is needed for
the different seasons of the year.

The breezes from the Atlantic, coming over the warm Gulf
Stream, are surcharged with moisture, and thus give Ireland
perhaps the dampest climate of any large body of land in the
world. The worst feature of this is that there is constant moisture without rain. It is said that a piece of wet leather, if left in
a room in summer, where there is not fire or sun, will not dry in
a month. The weather is cloudy to a degree unknown in most
lands. There are also frequent showers. But the average fall of
rain is about thirty inches a year, which does not differ much
from that of Central New York. Thunder storms, heavy rains
and prolonged frosts are of rare occurrence.

The prevalent soil is a fertile loam, resting on a rocky sub-
stratum, chiefly of limestone. The luxuriance of the pastures
and the heavy crops of oats raised even with the most wretched
cultivation attest the extraordinary fertility of the soil and geniality
of the climate. The depth, though in general not great, is in
some parts such as to admit of fresh vegetable mould being re-
peatedly thrown up by deeper ploughing, not unlike some soils in
our great western prairies. Even where the soil is thin, it yields
· richly, owing to the constant moisture of the climate. In an
extraordinarily dry season the crops on this thin soil fail. The
greatest and almost the only danger to the crops, however, is the
liability of the climate to long continued, excessive moisture,
owing to which the crops may not ripen, or cannot be harvested
when ripe.

The general surface of the country is plain. Yet low hills are
interspersed throughout the island. These rise at times almost
to mountain ranges, but not of such hight as to precipitate
great quantities of the moisture which is held in suspension by
the breeze from the Atlantic.

Ireland contains thirty-two thousand square miles. This is a little more than the State of Maine, or about two-thirds the State of New York, or four-fifths the State of Ohio. About two-thirds of the entire surface is reported as arable land. One-seventh of the surface is bog land.

The mineral wealth of Ireland is not unimportant. Several valuable coal fields exist; yet these do not produce enough to supply even the limited manufactures of the island, over a million tons a year being imported from England. Ireland is reported to contain much lead, copper and iron, but notwithstanding many attempts to work the metallic mines few have been found to repay the outlay. Still some of the copper mines have been found quite remunerative. Silver, tin and gold are also found, but not in very workable quantity. Other minerals, useful in manufactures and arts, and found in various parts of the island in remunerative quantities, are manganese, antimony, nickel, alum, porcelain, and brick clays, building-stone, marble, flag-stones and roofing slates. Valuable mineral springs abound in many parts of the island. The mineral wealth is, on the whole, very greatly inferior, however, to that of England.

The coast of Ireland is deeply indented with bays. If the possession of fine harbors would make a country great as a commercial and maritime power, she would be second to no country in Europe. The western shore is specially rich in harbors, though but one first-class natural harbor exists on the eastern shore towards England.

The coasts of Ireland abound with fish. The innumerable bays and mouths of rivers and creeks are the resort of vast shoals of herring, cod, ling, hake, mackerel and other varieties of fish.

The population of Ireland at the time of the Roman invasion of England appears to have been very small. Tacitus quotes Agricola as estimating that a single Roman legion would suffice to conquer the island. At the close of the devastating wars of the reign of Queen Elizabeth, Lord Montjoy's secretary asserts that not more than about a half million inhabitants escaped the edge of the sword or the horrors of famine. The first re-

liable estimate was made in 1652, since which time the census
returns have given the population as follows:

1652	850,000
1712	2,099,094
1788	4,040 000
1805	5,395,456
1821	6,801,827
1831	7,767,401
1841	8,175,124
1851	6,552,386
1861	5,798,564
1871	5,402,729

We have seen in English journals the present population of
Ireland estimated at a little over five and a half millions. The
maximum was reached in 1846, when it was towards nine millions. This was the most dense population in the known world.
Even now Ireland, as a rural country, is only rivaled, or equaled,
in the denseness of its population, by some provinces in China.

At the present time the population of Ireland is over three
times as dense, and in 1841 it was over four or five times as
dense, as the present population of the State of New York, ex-
cluding the cities of New York and Brooklyn, which form, strictly
speaking, the metropolis of the entire United States. In 1846
there were as many as 350 persons to each square mile of
arable land, which gives less than an average of two acres of
cultivated land to each person.

The rapid diminution of population since 1846 has been owing
to the failure of crops for several successive years, and the consequent terrible famine which reached its climax in 1848 and
swept away large numbers by absolute starvation, and to the
subsequent emigration of great numbers to England, the United
States, Canada and Australia. The number of Irishmen in
England is estimated at two millions; in the United States at
over four millions; in Canada and Australia at from a half million to a million. Thus there probably are fourteen or fifteen millions of people of Irish descent in the entire world. This
is an enormous increase from the eight hundred and fifty thousand
of only two hundred and thirty years ago.

The Irish are at the present time a mixed race. The original inhabitants were of Celtic origin, being allied to the Highland Scotch, the Welsh, the ancient Britons and the present inhabitants of Brittany in France. Of the 6,553,386 inhabitants in 1851, 219,-602 could speak only the Irish language; 1,204,684 could speak English and Irish ; most of the remainder could speak English only. A portion of the inhabitants of Ulster in the North of Ireland are of Scotch descent ; some thousands are of German origin ; and perhaps a half million or more are of English birth or descent.

In religion the vast majority are Roman Catholic. By the census of 1871 the population was thus divided ; Roman Catholic, 4,150,877 ; Protestant, 1,260,568; Jews, 258. Of the Protestant, nearly one-half belong to the Church of England ; about the same number belong to the Presbyterian Church, and a limited number are Wesleyan Methodists and Independents.

ARTICLE II.

THE EARLY HISTORY OF IRELAND.

It is one of the most firmly established facts in history that race characteristics exist. The qualities and attributes of ancestors are continued to their descendants to " thousands of generations." As the history of a people progresses, new influences are developed from within or are added from without, and thus there results finally that collection of qualities which are grouped under the one term of "national character."

The mass of the Irish people are undoubtedly of Celtic origin. This is shown by the names of rivers, towns, mountains and other historic objects throughout the island ; and by the tumuli, cairns, cromlechs, druidical circles and other archæological relics which have triumphed over the ravages of centuries and remain to attest the relationship of the early inhabitants. The very name " Erin," the most ancient appellation of the island, and that to which the natives cling with the greatest veneration, is derived from the Celtic "Iar" or " Eir," which signifies " *Western*." Ireland was probably known to the ancient Phœnicians. The Greeks gave it the name of " Ierna," and gave it the third

rank in size of all the islands of the world, placing only Great
Britain and Ceylon before it.   The Romans called it " Hibernia."
The ancient Britons named it " Iverdon," and the early Saxons
" Ierland" or " Ireland," the " *Land of the West.*" Strabo, writing in the first century before Christ, places Ireland north of
Britain.   He is able to mention nothing further of the inhabitants than that they were cannibals, and that the men held it
very noble to devour their own parents when old, and had no
aversion to marry their own sisters and mothers.   Ptolemy, writing 150 A. D., describes the coasts of Ireland as being inhabited
by various tribes, but he was ignorant of the inhabitants of the
interior.

The Irish annalists, basing their accounts upon the romantic
fables of their bards, give their country a history, reaching far
back, to the very beginnings, indeed, of human history.   From
this mass of mythical legend a few probable facts can be traced.
A curious legend attaches to " Jacob's Stone."   Tradition says
that this was cherished by one of the Early Irish tribes, with the
belief that sovereignty would remain with that tribe or nation
whose king was crowned with it.   This stone, after having been
preserved many generations by the Milesian kings, was taken to
Scotland and there fraudulently detained by one of these kings.
It was used in crowning the Scotch kings, until the time of
Edward I. of England, who on his conquest of Scotland, transferred it, with all of the appendages of royalty, to London,
where it is still kept under the name of " Jacob's Stone," and is
used in the ceremonial of the crowning of the kings of Great
Britain, much as the Iron Crown of Lombardy is used in crowning the Italian kings.

Another legend relates that Milesius, an Ibero-Celtic hero
from Spain, landed in Ireland and subjugated the country.   The
son of Milesius established his capital at Tarah.   To him most
of the ancient illustrious Irish families claim to trace their origin.
The last lineal descendant of this dynasty claiming title to the
throne of Ireland is said to have died in 1198.   The usual fate
of these sovereigns was to die at the hand of sons, brothers, or
others upon whom the inheritance of the throne might be liable
to fall.

Towards the end of the fourth century, some Irish and Scotch tribes, which have been named the Picts and Scots, made incursions into the Roman possessions in England. The leader of a rival faction invited Agricola to invade and conquer Ireland. But the many troubles of the Roman Empire forbade further projects of conquest. The name of "Scotia Major" was applied to Ireland, and of "Scotia Novia" to Scotland, by some historians. The interchange of names between the peoples and the countries of Ireland and Scotland, concerning their early history, was a fruitful source of dispute between Irish and Scotch writers in the sixteenth and following centuries, and it can hardly be said that the contest is entirely at an end now.

At the beginning of the fifth century, Pope Celestine sent Palladius to Ireland, to convert the Pagan inhabitants to Christianity. Others had preceded him. But neither their labors nor his produced permanent results. This was reserved for a Scotchman named Succath, who afterwards received the Christian name of Patrick, whose remarkable successes, extending through a life of unusual length, have given him the title of the "Apostle of Ireland." The chieftain of Ulster was his first convert. Soon the king, Logary, on hearing Patrick preach to the assembled court at Tarah, pronounced himself a convert. Many subjects followed his example. Patrick founded a school of theology at Armagh, which soon became so famous that students flocked thither from all countries of Europe. At one time seven thousand were said to have been under instruction there. Patrick's successors founded similar schools in other cities, which retained their fame until the eighth century, and sent forth Christian apostles to Scotland, England and many countries of the continent of Europe. So famous were the theological schools, monasteries and other educational establishments of Ireland that this country acquired in the Christian world the title of "Island of the Saints" or "Holy Island." Missionaries from Ireland founded many famous ecclesiastical establishments in the countries they visited, extending their work as far as France, Switzerland, Austria and Italy itself.

To this, the most brilliant period of Irish learning, is to be attributed the peculiar style of art-ornamentation of illuminated

manuscripts and other works, which was for a long time attributed to the Anglo-Saxons, who were indebted to the Irish mainly
for Christianity and entirely for letters. This brilliant progress
of civilization in Ireland was checked by the invasion of the
Scandinavians, which continued from the end of the eighth to
the beginning of the eleventh century. Already in the seventh
century King Egfried, of Northumbria, in England, had made
a disastrous incursion into Ireland, to punish the attacks of the
Irish upon Anglesea, Mona and England. The Danes and Nor-
mans then continued their piratical incursions, and at times held
the entire island under severe and cruel domination.

The work of St. Patrick and his followers did not convert
Ireland, however, into a spiritual paradise. The brief notices
of the civil and political condition of the country which are
extant refer to a repetition of the turbulence, desolation and
crime which had marked the long preceding era of paganism.
The only event of importance, that does not refer to domestic
commotion and foreign warfare, was a convention held at Drum-
keath for the purpose of curbing the license and profligacy of
the bards, which had become intolerable. This evil was merely
diminished, however, by limiting the number of the bards, whose
profligacy for many centuries was one of the chief means of cor-
rupting the youth of both sexes. Continued commotion and
incessant civil strife racked the country through the eleventh and
part of the twelfth century.

The Anglo-Saxons, who at this time were ruling in England,
had little connection with Ireland, their projects for invasion and
conquest being turned rather to the continent. The Bishop of
Dublin, however, acknowledged the spiritual supremacy of the
Archbishop of Canterbury. When a synod was held at Armagh,
in 1170, to inquire into the cause of the arrival of the English
for conquest, the impending calamity was attributed to the sins of
the people, and more especially to the practice of buying English children and selling them for slaves. Giraldus Cambrensis,
in stating the fact, adds "that the English, by a common vice of
their country, had a custom of selling their children and kinsfolk
into Ireland, although not driven to it by extreme poverty."

The king of Leinster, by his tyranny, had incurred the hatred of his own subjects and of the other Irish princes and chiefs, and he was driven from his dominion. He had recourse for assistance to Henry II of England, under whom he offered to hold his crown as tributary, if restored by that monarch's exertions. This offer was very acceptable to Henry, who had long turned his thoughts to the acquisition of Ireland. As early as 1154 he had procured a bull from Pope Adrian, who owed his election to Henry's influence, conferring upon Henry the sovereignty of Ireland, "in order to its civilization," upon payment of Peter's pence to the court of Rome. With the assistance of Welsh adventurers, Henry's general accomplished the subjection of Ireland. The Irish chieftains assembled at Lismore in a great council or parliament, and received and swore to live by English laws. A synod of the clergy was also held at Cashel, who adopted for their future regulation the rules and doctrines of the English Church. After several revolts and renewed subjugations of the Irish by their new rulers, Roderic, the last Irish king, died in 1198, in the monastery of Cong, at the unusual age of a hundred and twenty years. Thus was inaugurated the rule of the English in Ireland which has lasted seven hundred years, and now leaves Ireland in the turbulent condition in which we find it to-day.

ARTICLE III.

HISTORY OF IRELAND FROM THE ENGLISH CONQUEST TO THE REFORMATION.

We have thus traced the history of Ireland down to the beginning of the English domination. Originally Ireland was occupied by a large number of tribes, which were ruled by chieftains, much like the clans of Scotland, or the tribes of Albania, in Turkey, at the present day. The two descendants of the Iberian invader, Milesius, divided Ireland into two parts, by a line running east and west, from Dublin to Galway. These divisions were called Leath Conn and Leath Mogha, or Conn's share and Mogha's share, names that are yet familiarly given by the Irish to the northern and southern part of the island. A later division into the five petty kingdoms of Leinster, Ulster, Munster, Connaught and Meath continued until after the English invasion, though the last of the lineal descendants of Milesius, having a claim upon the throne of Ireland, Roderic, died in 1198. After the time of King John, (A. D. 1200), the country was divided into two parts. These were known as " Ireland within the Pale," or the part around Dublin where the English held direct sway ; and " Ireland without the Pale," or the remainder of the country where the sway was more indirect. The limits of the "Pale" varied greatly at different times, according as the native chieftains were more or less orderly or seditious, and as the English were able to send troops to hold the country in subjection. In the time of King John the Pale included about one-third of the island. Outside of the Pale his authority was merely nominal.

King John ordained that the English laws should be introduced bodily into Ireland, with all their judicial forms. The sons of Roderic soon engaged in fearful contention over the portion of the Kingdom of Connaught which Henry had left to Roderic when he submitted to the English rule, thus repeating the intestine turmoil which has ever devastated the island.

Immediately after the accession of Henry III, in 1216, the Irish sent to this King a list of the encroachments which had been made upon their rights, with a petition to be taken under royal protection. Henry sent them in reply a copy of the Magna Charta, placing them on the same footing with the English subjects. During Henry's reign Ireland was placed under supervision of his youngest son, Edward, and sank into a most wretched condition, the part within the Pale being torn by the hostilities of the rival English barons. The Irish people were dreadfully oppressed by the arrogant tyranny of these feudal lords. The chief-justice's plea to the King for not suppressing these disorders was that he " deemed it expedient to suffer one knave to destroy another, to save expense to the King !" The King was satisfied with this evasive answer. The wars and tumults of the barons continued to be tolerated, and the Irish who wished to secure the protection of English laws were forced to procure it at great cost, the fees enriching the judges. Edward II made an impulsive effort to restore the royal authority and to suppress the exorbitant power of the English barons. But soon the royal mandates were defied, and the private wars of the Irish chieftains without the Pale, and of the English barons within it, were resumed without constraint.

After the battle of Bannockburn, Robert Bruce, King of Scotland, purposed to detach Ireland from England and to attach it to Scotland. In 1315 a large army of Scotch soldiers entered Ireland, and Bruce was crowned King of Ireland. Feidlim, King of Connaught, who was opposing the Scotch, was attacked by the English troops and slain. With him perished the last hope of restoring the Irish monarchy. After many successes Bruce met with a disastrous defeat by the English forces, and the Scotch forces were withdrawn from Ireland.

No relief came to the Irish people by the expulsion of the Scotch. On the contrary, Edward III, after hearing favorably the petition of the suffering Irish, attempted in vain, by energetic measures, to restore order. Parts of Leinster, Ulster and Meath had been confiscated and yielded with almost sovereign power to the descendants of former generals. Edward extended this policy to other parts. In consequence a few powerful chieftains, or feudal rulers, were able to overawe the law, and throw the country into convulsions by their mutual contests for superiority. The chief governor finally called for a large force of troops to re-establish the king's authority. As means were lacking to defray even the living expenses of the soldiers, the troops were quartered in the country "in coygne and livery." This consisted in "taking man's meat, horse's meat and money" of all the inhabitants, at the will of the soldier. This extortion was copied from the Irish method of paying their soldiers, who received no other pay. However this may have worked with the Irish tribes or clans, under the English rule in Ireland it became "the heaviest oppression that ever was inflicted upon any kingdom, Christian or heathen."

Another remarkable blindness and folly seemed to have struck the English government with reference to this distressed province. An order was issued that all public officers whose property existed wholly in Ireland should be displaced, and persons born in England and having lands in England should replace them. The displaced officials were naturally greatly irritated and exasperated at this wholesale and tyrannical procedure. They began to attach themselves to the Irish by marriage and community of interest, and became "more bitterly Irish than the Irish themselves."

A new Lord-Lieutenant was sent to Ireland. He forbade any of the "old English" or of the King's subjects by Irish birth to approach his camp. A parliament, or assemblage of notables, was held at Kilkenny, and the famous "Kilkenny statute" was proclaimed. This forms one of the greatest political epochs in the history of Ireland. This statute enacted that marriage, fostering, "gossipred" (being sponsor of a child in baptism) was declared treasonable ; conformity to Irish law was punished in the same way ; the use of Irish names, language or apparel, by any person of English birth or descent was punishable by imprisonment or the forfeiture of lands. Penalties were imposed on those who permitted their Irish neighbors to graze on their lands, who admitted them as members into ecclesiastical houses, or who gave encouragement to Irish bards, musicians or story-tellers. The execution of this statute was enforced by the anathemas of the church against its violators ! The distractions of the country greatly increased. The English rule was practically limited to the portion of the Pale immediately contiguous to Dublin.

During the reign of Henry IV, the Scotch made another invasion into Ireland and acquired some possession from which they were never wholly removed. The border districts of the Pale were harrassed by the Irish chieftains, and were only able to purchase immunity from invasion by the payment of tribute, called "black rent."

The English Parliament now passed a most impolitic law, requiring all the Irish to quit England. Some time after this the Lord-Lieutenant, Kildare, having overcome a powerful insurrection of the Irish and the "degenerate English," allowed his troops to commit the most terrible excesses, refusing to give quarter to the enemy and continuing the massacre until nightfall.

A period now arrived when religion appeared as an element in the troubles between England and Ireland. It will be noticed that in giving the sovereignty of Ireland to England, and in all the issues between these countries, the popes and the Church of Rome had thrown their power and influence on the side of England.

Henry VIII determined to extend to Ireland the Reformation which he had established so easily and so firmly in England. A parliament, assembled at the suggestion of Browne, the first Protestant Archbishop of Dublin, acknowledged the King's supremacy in the fullest manner. It forbade appeals to Rome and removed the authority of the Romish See. An act was passed to found schools in every parish for teaching the natives the English language and the rudiments of useful knowledge. It is strange to say that the country became so tranquilized and loyal to the English throne that Francis I, King of France, then at war with England, failed to move the Irish to insurrection. On the contrary, large numbers of Irish joined the English army to invade France, and fought with desperate valor.

ARTICLE IV.

HISTORY OF IRELAND FROM THE REFORMATION TO THE TIME OF THE GEORGES.

The auspicious inauguration of the Reformation in Ireland and of lenient and equal government to all classes of subjects was destined to be short-lived and futile. The Irish clergy in general opposed a change of religion, and incurred the wrath of the impetuous Henry. The Catholic clergy were removed with violence and acrimony. Most inveterate hostilities were engendered and most desolating wars harrassed the island. Large tracts of the country were converted into deserts, and the miserable remnants of the population were forced to feed upon grass or the filthiest garbage. The estates of many insurgent lords were attainted and vast properties were forfeited to the crown.

Nearly the whole of Ulster, in the northern part of Ireland, passing thus into the hands of the King of England, he resolved to remodel this province, by removing the ancient owners and replacing them by a colony of English and Scotch settlers. Estates varying in size from one to two thousand acres each were portioned out, the proprietors binding themselves to build substantial houses and to people them with English and Scotch tenantry. Thus was established the Protestant population of North Ireland. The city of London and many corporations and guilds took large tracts of this land and hold it to this day.

Under the plea of justice a commission was formed to discover defective titles to estates. Since many records and deeds were lost during those turbulent times, vast numbers of objectionable owners of property were ejected in the most arbitrary manner. A portion of the land thus confiscated was given to informants or discoverers of defective titles. By this process over a half million acres passed to the crown. Strafford, the Lord-Lieutenant under Charles I, subverted the titles of many Catholic proprietors in Connaught and replaced them by Protestants, sending troops to overawe the juries when the titles were examined. Strafford also gave great encouragement to the linen manufactories in Ulster, which have ever since flourished so prosperously.

To repress insurrections in Ireland during the Commonwealth, Cromwell entered the island with a large army. By a vigorous and, indeed, merciless policy he quickly overcame all opposition. The greater part of the Irish gentry and nobility and of the army in Ireland had expatriated themselves, and their estates were apportioned to loyal contributors to the expenses of the army of subjugation, and to the soldiers who had not received full pay for services.

These confiscations finally included the greater part of the surface of Ireland. Private soldiers and desperate adventurers often became owners of large estates which had previously belonged to native families of ancient descent or to the newer Anglo-Irish nobility. The impoverished descendants of these former owners of the soil of Ireland now constitute one of the most turbulent elements in the population of that island.

A series of severe repressive laws, called the " Penal Code," was ordained, to restrict the rights and privileges of the Catholics. Thus under it no Catholic was, under any condition, to remain in a town or within a certain space around it. The com-

moner sort were prohibited from quitting their place of residence
without permission. The Catholic inhabitants of peaceable
counties were assessed for injuries done to Protestant property in
other counties. It was forbidden for more than ten Catholics to
assemble together. Priests of parishes in which meetings were
held were transported to penal colonies. Acts were also passed
forbidding Catholics to educate their children at home or abroad,
except under Protestant teachers or tutors. Catholics could not
become tutors without special license. A Catholic could not become guardian to a child whose parents had conformed. A
Catholic could not hold lands for longer than thirty-one years.
A Catholic could not inherit lands from a Protestant relation. A
Catholic could not qualify for office or vote at an election without first performing an oath of abjuration. These and other
severe laws kept the Catholic population in a state of despera-
tion. They are characterized by Burke as "the very acme of
political persecution."

The same violent bigotry which enacted this Penal Code
against the Catholics was soon directed against the Non-conformists, who, under the Commonwealth, made up the body of the
colonists in the north of Ireland. The Calvinist chapels were
closed. The ministers were imprisoned. The Puritan population was not permitted to hold office of any kind, unless they
submitted to the English Established Church. With a consent
almost universal the stern Puritan colonists sold their grants to
English speculators, and sought a more congenial home in New
England, where their grandchildren a century later gave England cause to regret the prelatical zeal that sent them thither.
A revival of this persecution of the Non-Conformists took place
fifty years afterwards. Again many of the small landholders sold
out to the owners of larger estates, and took flight to the New
World. Ireland thus lost a valuable part of its population ; the
number of small landed proprietors was diminished ; and acces-
sions were made again to the liberty-loving colonists of America.

In all this the prelatical Protestantism of England did not sin
beyond the age. Roman Catholicism was equally and even more
fiercely proscriptive in other lands, where it held sway, as in
France, Spain and Austria. The fugitive Puritans in New Eng-

land were themselves not prepared to exercise political liberty. But the memories of the Penal Code remain in Ireland to-day a most rankling element of disturbance.

The principle that British colonies existed only for the benefit of the mother country, which in its milder applications caused the separation and independence of the American colonies, was applied with intensified and exasperating severity, and with disastrous consequences, to Ireland, which was near to England and lay at its mercy. After the war of the Restoration had closed, Ireland began to recuperate. The commercial spirit of monopoly of the English manufacturers, who had long viewed with a jealous eye the increase of the woolen manufacture in Ireland, to which the cheapness of living and the excellency of the pasturage afforded peculiar advantages, prevailed in influencing the king to make a solemn assurance that he would do everything possible to discourage that manufacture, adding as a mitigation that every encouragement should be afforded to the linen manufacture. The former part of the promise was rigidly adhered to ; the latter was disregarded. Every attempt to establish the linen manufacture in the South of Ireland failed, chiefly from the opposition of the clergy to the introduction of an equitable mode for tithing the flax. An act of Parliament was passed prohibiting the exportation of wool or woolens from Ireland to other countries than England, and the price was fixed at which wool should be sold to the English. The exportation of fuller's earth to Ireland was prohibited. With the best wool crop in Europe, and with unlimited water power, Ireland thus soon made barely woolen goods enough for the poorer classes of her own population.

The forests of Ireland furnished excellent timber for ship building. The harbors of Cork and Dublin began to be filled with vessels built in Ireland and manned by Irish sailors. Droves of Irish cattle were landed in Bristol. Irish bacon and butter, and even Irish grain, made its way to the English markets. All this threatened the English farmers with ruin, just as the importation of American cattle, meat, butter and grain is now threatening English farmers with ruin. The extension of the Navigation Act at this time ruined Irish shipping. The exportation of cattle or provisions to England was soon afterwards prohibited. Even when the Irish Parliament, through a wish to alleviate the suffering caused by the great fire in London, in 1666, sent to that city a free gift of thirty thousand cattle, the only wealth of the country at that time, the well-intentioned donation was rejected as an attempt to evade the law under the mask of benevolence.

Irish industry was deliberately destroyed. Industrious habits, then, as now, the one great remedy for the temporal woes of Ireland, were mercilessly blighted at the outset, and the mass of the people were condemned to an inheritance of poverty, out of which no effort of their own could lift them.

The Irish State Church, a branch of the Protestant Anglican Church, was made an instrument of the greatest injustice. The Church in Ireland became a receptacle for persons whom English ministers wished to promote, but did not dare to promote at home. Swift's story of the highwayman who killed the bishops elect, stole their letters patent, and were consecrated in their places, is no very extreme caricature. Even within the present century a prime minister wished to give an Irish bishopric to the younger son of a noble family. The Irish primate objected, declaring that the young man's character was notoriously infamous, and that he would rather resign than consecrate him. Yet the English cabinet persisted. The primate's scruples were in some way overcome, and the young man of notoriously infamous character was forced upon the bench of bishops.

In other ways, too, Ireland was used as a convenience. Ireland had a pension list, for services honorably distinguished. On this list are found the names of royal mistresses, favorites, poor foreign relations, or corrupt officials, whose services had been bought. This was a frequent subject of complaint in the Irish Parliament. The complainant was generally silenced by being made a recipient of polluted bounty. The Viceroy's letters for nearly a century contain reports, at the close of each session, of the members of the two Irish houses who had been corrupted, and of the terms which had been paid.

The abominable injustices and oppressions which England exercised over Ireland during this period, and which were continued afterwards until the present century, some of them not being corrected indeed at the present day, make one's blood tingle at the mere reading. A thousandth part of the wrongs which Ireland has suffered at the hands of England would be deemed sufficient to justify a people in rising in desperate revolt against such odious misrule.

ARTICLE V.

IRELAND FROM THE TIME OF GEORGE II UNTIL THE DISSOLUTION OF THE IRISH PARLIAMENT, A. D. 18co.

The operation of the Penal Code, while it enslaved the Catholics, pauperized the country. The great mass of the population was deprived of the main stimulus to industry, the hope of improving their condition by their own exertions. The great landed proprietors found their lands decreasing in value, from the neglect of agricultural improvement. The degradation of the Catholics reached its lowest point in a case where one of that faith was gravely told in a court of justice that the law did not recognize the existence of a papist.

A state of society so anomalous, in which universal liberty was the avowed principle of the British government, yet whose slavery, unmitigated by the protection which sordid interest extends to the preservation of individual property, was the practice, could not but be most precarious. The government became aware of the dangers, through the threat of the young Pretender to the crown of England to invade Ireland. Lord Chesterfield was sent over in the spirit of conciliation to ward off the threatened danger. An accidental circumstance gave this astute diplomat occasion to inaugurate the amelioration of the condition of the Catholics, which has continued to the present day. The Catholics had held their assemblies for religious worship in the most secluded places. The rewards offered by the laws for the detection of their priests, or of those who attended their ceremonies, compelled them to the strictest secrecy. The floor of a building in one of the narrowest streets of Dublin, where mass was being celebrated, gave way, and caused the death or mutilation of a number of the wretched beings who had there assembled to worship in the way in which they had been trained. Lord Chesterfield, with the tact which characterized him in the annals of fashionable society, seized the opportunity to declare that he would not be a party to a religious system liable to the hazard of such results.

The accession of George III was seized upon by the Catholics to present appeals for the alleviance of the injustices of the Penal Code. At this time some vital change was needed in the administration of the country. The revenue was declining, and the peasantry were every year becoming more destitute and discontented. The wretched sufferers, attributing their misery to the exaction of tithes and the enclosure of many lands hitherto left open in commonage, banded themselves together in large bodies at night and destroyed the new enclosures. These depredators were called " Whiteboys," from their wearing white shirts over their clothes, to be known to each other in their nocturnal expeditions. They proceeded also to attack persons obnoxious to them, particularly the tithe proctors, treating with barbarous cruelty those who fell into their hands. The British government retaliated by a body of severe and arbitrary repressive laws, known as the Whiteboy Acts, many of which are still in force. The landholders were won over to the side of the government by giving them more of the offices of trust and profit, and by indulging their enmity against the Catholics, who were still suspected of being cemented in secret union for the recovery of their forfeited estates.

The severity of the Whiteboy Acts caused a temporary cessation of insubordination in one part of the country, only to give vent to it in another part. The disturbances in the South of Ireland have been imputed to Catholic conspiracy, aided by foreign, mostly French, influence. But a similar systematized spirit of outrage now displayed itself in the northern part of Ulster, which was chiefly inhabited by a Protestant population. The real and immediate cause of the outbreak was the same in both parts of the country. High rents and the rapacity of the agents of the absentee landlords drove the people to insurrection. The revolters in Ulster took the name of " Hearts of Steel." Emigration to the American colonies was the consequence of the depressed state of the peasantry and the severe laws enacted against them. The war with these colonies, by closing this vent for the discharge of the discontented population, caused the elements of disturbance to increase at home. The war against the revolting colonies in America also closed the trade of Ireland, America having been the great market for Irish linen, the sole thriving branch of Irish manufacturers. An embargo was also laid on the export of provisions from Ireland, in favor of some great English contractors. The people of Ireland now began to retaliate against the severity of the English restrictions to Irish industry, by banding together to confine themselves to the use of their own manufactures.

When the French revolution broke out, the Protestants began to call more loudly for reform, and the Catholics to press more openly for admission into the pale of the constitution. Some reforms were granted. Meantime fierce and deadly contention broke out between the peasantry of opposite religious creeds in the northern and central counties of Ireland. The Catholics first took the name of " Defenders." Afterwards they joined the party which had been formed to effect a separation from the British crown, and were called the " United Irishmen." The Protestants took the name of " Orangemen." The feuds between these two parties have not yet subsided. They have been carried across wide oceans, and have broken out in turmoil and riots wherever the Irish emigrants have settled, in Canada, the United States and Australia.

The feud between these parties soon showed itself by acts of augmented atrocity on both sides. The means of aggression adopted by the " Defenders" consisted in nocturnal plunder, house-burnings and murders. The Orangemen, backed by the sanction of the government, had recourse to statutes of increased rigor, and to military violence beyond the law. The " United Irishmen" having invited the French to invade Ireland, as was supposed, the government had recourse to still stronger measures to put down the spirit of insurrection. The *habeas corpus* act was suspended. Domiciliary visits throughout the rural parts were frequent. Meetings of the people were dispersed by violence. Torture was inflicted to enforce confession from suspected persons. Large bodies of soldiers were allowed to live at free quarters in suspected districts. The relaxation of discipline and consequent outrages caused General Abercrombie to declare, in general orders to the troops, that "the army was in a state of licentiousness which rendered it formidable to every one but the enemy." General Lake was sent to replace the outspoken Abercrombie. By his commands the soldiers exercised an almost uncontrolled authority, in which they were sanctioned by instructions from the government empowering the army to use force at the discretion of the officers against the people.

The United Irishmen finally, in 1778, organized an open rebellion. This rebellion was repressed by the British troops. The operations of the army were attended at times by severe and almost merciless rigor. In some cases no quarter was given to Irish troops after they had surrendered unconditionally. These military operations were seconded by most violent acts on the part of the civil government. Numbers of persons arrested on suspicion were tied up, and flogged, to extort confession. In the rural regions more refined forms of agony were adopted to elicit discovery or to gratify revenge. In some cases they hanged up their victim and let him down again just before life was extinct, thus prolonging and repeating the sufferings of strangulation. On the heads of others they applied caps lined with heated pitch, which, when fastened on and allowed to cool, were suddenly torn off, carrying with them the hair and skin. In the spirit of fiendish mockery they cut ridges in the hair of others in the form of a cross, and, filling up the furrows with gunpowder, set fire to it. In two cases, companies of suspected persons, some of them respectable farmers, being arrested on suspicion, were deliberately shot, without even the form of a trial, lest they should join the rebel forces when the troops were removed. In retaliation for this barbarous method of carrying on warfare and of administering justice, the insurgents put to death by the sword, the pike and the musket many hundred prisoners from among the British troops, who were charged with having exercised these atrocities upon the Irish insurgents.

The rebellion of 1798 was made the occasion for dissolving the Parliament of Great Britain and Ireland, and uniting them in one Imperial Parliament. "The Union broke the strength of the aristocracy [in Ireland]; it untied the hands of the government; it loosened the dependence of the government upon a single party, and restored to the State the privilege of good government. Ireland, in fact, for centuries possessed but two classes of society, the rich and the poor. There was no solid bond between the crown and the people. The feudalism which the religion of Luther in England and that of Calvin in Scotland had tended much to annihilate flourished in most parts of Erin in all its dessolating vigor."

The Act of Union did not produce at once the results promised by its advocates. It neither tranquilized the country nor aided its material prosperity. The Protestant aristocracy found their influence diminished by it. The Catholics soon discovered the hopelessness of securing through this means a removal of their political disabilities. Unfortunately a rash and futile attempt at organized rebellion was made three years after the Union was effected, under the leadership of Robert Emmett, which not only retarded the approach of the era of good feeling, but also was the occasion of renewed vigilance by the Imperial Government, which held Ireland more completely in its power than when Ireland had a separate parliament of its own. Notwithstanding all this, the climax was passed in the griefs and wrongs which Ireland had suffered from the hands of England during a long period of seven centuries.

ARTICLE VI.

THE INDUSTRIAL AND AGRICULTURAL CONDITION OF IRELAND.

We have thus traced the salient points in the history of Ireland which have relation to the origin and development of the troubles which are at present agitating that country. We saw Ireland soon after the fall of the Roman Empire and the introduction of Christianity into northern Europe become in the seventh and eighth centuries the center of Christian education and of general culture north of the Alps. We then saw the island torn by intestine feuds and wars, and finally delivered to the rule of the

English kings, through the treachery of Irish rulers and by the sanction and authority of the Pope of Rome. Then followed seven hundred years of arbitrary and cruel rule by England, during which the antagonisms of race, religion, class distinctions and commercial interests were all turned to the injury of the Irish people. The lands were several times confiscated almost bodily and delivered to new classes of owners. The whole dreary history reads more like the rule of an Asiatic despot over a conquered and helpless race, than like the rule of an enlightened Christian nation over a province within sight of its very shores.

With the close of the last century the misery and degradation of Ireland reached its lowest point. Since the close of the Napoleonic wars, more especially, constant agitation has produced many changes, which have greatly ameliorated the legal condition and relations of the Irish people.

In the year 1829 the famous Penal Code, which included the disabilities and special penalties against the Roman Catholics, was abolished. Thenceforward Catholics were allowed to sit in Parliament and to hold civil or administrative offices. In 1833 the foundation was laid for a system of national education, which is supported by grants of public money for the education of the poor without distinction of religious creed. In 1869 a Land Act was passed, greatly restricting the powers of landlords, especially as to the arbitrary eviction of tenants. In 1870 the Anglican Church was disestablished. All governmental restrictions to the development of agricultural, manufacturing or commercial industry have been removed. Actual governmental aid has been proffered to promote the fisheries and other sources of wealth. It is but just to say that at present no disposition is manifested by the British Government or the British Parliament to deal otherwise than justly, honorably and generously with Ireland in all those points where the government at the present day can touch the evils which have been inherited from the seven hundred years of previous misrule of this distressed island.

As will be readily seen, however, many of the evils and wrongs from which the people in Ireland at the present day are suffering are of such a nature that they can never be righted. In this Ireland is not peculiar. History is full of examples where races, nations, communities and individuals suffer unjustly, by inheritance, from wrongs which never can be righted. To chafe and writhe under wrongs done to ancestors five, ten or twenty generations ago is only folly.

Many of the descendants of the former owners of confiscated estates in Ireland have for ages and centuries gone through the form of conveying by will these confiscated estates to their children or legal heirs, though these hypothetical owners are living in the most abject poverty and misery, as have their ancestors before them through all these weary centuries. This futile effort to keep up the form of legal ownership to vast and valuable estates is to-day an important factor among the general disturbing elements in the land troubles which have so long agitated this island, and which are now so pre-eminently occupying the attention of the British Parliament and government.

What we have thus seen of the antecedent history of Ireland may thus explain to a large degree the present poverty and misery of the people of this beautiful but unfortunate island. The contrast between the agricultural, manufacturing and commercial prosperity of England and Scotland and the poverty and misery of Ireland forms one of the most painful pictures that meet the eye of the traveler in Europe. How to correct the present low economical condition of Ireland is a problem to-day which taxes the astuteness of the most able of British political economists and statesmen.

Let us glance at some of the details of the wretched condition of industry in Ireland. In the first place, as we said in our first article, the coasts of Ireland abound with fish, which might form a most remunerative source of wealth, and go a great way to prevent the ever-threatening famine which so frequently ravages that island. Yet, despite an annual bounty by the government of five thousand pounds for the encouragement of fisheries, the number of men and boats employed in the fishing trade has decreased one-half within the last forty years. The government has finally withdrawn the bounty, as it produced no valuable results. Commissions of relief, in times of famine and distress, have found groups of starving men roaming listlessly along the shores of bays, whose waters teem with nourishing and palatable fish, literally starving in sight of food which they lacked the energy to capture.

The only important branch of manufactures in Ireland is that of linen, and this flourishes only in the northern portion, where a large population of orderly and skilled workmen render it safe for capital to seek investment in this industry.

The same conditions which have caused cotton to travel from Georgia to New England to be made into cloth cause wool to go from Ireland to England to be manufactured into cloth. There is in Central and Southern Ireland no population of skilled and industrious workmen to be employed in woolen manufactories. Also the cost of transportation of wool from Galway, Cork or Dublin to Liverpool or Lancaster is unimportant. And, further, the vast capital invested in woolen manufacture in England enables the capitalists there to crush out any rising industry in Ireland. It may be added that the prospect of being shot on his way home some fine evening, by some frenzied Irishman, is not a strong inducement to capitalists to enter upon the erection of factories in this turbulent country. Of other than woolen manufactures Ireland has practically none whatever. Her mining and commercial interests also are unimportant. There being thus no great manufacturing, mining or commercial centers, there is no home market for the surplus products of the soil. All agricultural products must seek a foreign market. They are transported mostly to Liverpool and Glasgow.

The vast majority of the population of Ireland is thus engaged in the cultivation of the soil. We approach, therefore, the great question upon which the agitations of this turbulent people have turned for the last fifty years, or since the repeal of the Penal Code in 1829.

As in England and Scotland, so in Ireland, almost the entire soil is held in very large estates. These estates are cut up into "holdings," or portions leased to separate tenants. In England and Scotland the farmers prefer to hire land rather than to own it. They do not purchase when the opportunity offers, but rather sell any land they may chance to own if favorable opportunity presents itself. The theory is that a farmer who has from one to five thousand pounds of capital and a thorough knowledge of farming is able to work a much larger farm than he can purchase. The large farmer, like the manufacturer, does no manual work on his farm. Like the cotton or woolen manufacturer, he uses his superior ability in superintendence, hiring mere laborers to do the manual work. The English farmers are, therefore, men of much business ability, and often rise to competency and even wealth, forming an important portion of the middle classes, which contribute so much to the stability of the English governmental and social system.

In Ireland the same general system of letting out the large estates of the landholders in holdings to tenants prevails as in England. The conditions of tenantry are in many respects very different, however, from those in England. One characteristic difference is in the size of the holdings. The land of Ireland is owned by 12,000 landlords. The number of holdings is about 600,000. These holdings are distributed in about the following proportions:

Size of Holdings.	Number of Holdings.	Average size in acres.
One acre or less	40,000	$\frac{2}{3}$ of an acre
1 to 5 acres,	84,000	3 acres.
5 " 15 "	180,000	10 "
15 " 30 "	140,000	22 "
30 " 50 "	70,000	40 "
50 " 100 "	55,000	74 "
100 " 200 "	21,000	153 "
200 " 500 "	8,500	355 "
Over 500 "	1,500	1,300 "

It will thus be seen that the Irish farmers are a very different class of persons from the English farmers. One-half of the holdings are less than ten acres in size, giving an average of about five or six acres to a holding. Only 31,000 of the holdings cover more than 100 acres apiece. Only 10,000 include over 200 acres. Thus only a very small proportion of the Irish tenant farmers cultivate their land on the same scale with the usual English farmer. On the other hand, the great majority of Irish tenant farmers have holdings which scarcely rise in size to the dignity of a respectable garden. This circumstance alone is sufficient to keep the Irish tenant continually in a precarious condition, as to procuring only a bare subsistence for his family, even if he owned the land of his holding. When to this is added the payment of rent, the tenant is in a chronic state of distress and of difficulty with his landlord. Let one or more unfavorable seasons diminish or ruin his crops, and he is in destitution and misery, if not threatened with starvation. Thus occurred the great famine of 1846–48. Thus occurred the great destitution and distress of the last two years. Thus ruin, distress and famine will continue to occur as long as this system of exceedingly small holdings is practiced.

The English landlord has the right to refuse to renew a lease to a tenant, when the lease expires. The lease in England is for a limited time, as from five to twenty-five years, the more usual term being ten or fifteen years. An English landlord can thus enlarge the holdings at will, or he can throw a holding into a park or cut it up into city or village lots.

By a traditional common law which has indeed been ratified in some regards by definite statute, in Ireland, a holding can be continued indefinitely if the tenant desires to renew it and pays the rent promptly. This places the Irish landlord at a great disadvantage, as to the profitable management of his estate. It also greatly embarrasses the renewal of a lease. An odious or unprofitable tenant cannot be displaced. The leases in Ireland·have frequently been very long, often extending over sixty or ninety years. In some cases they extend nine hundred and ninety-nine years, probably owing to the fear of dispute of title, when the estates were confiscated and sold to the new owners. These exceedingly long leases are a fruitful source of anti-rent disturbance.

The English farmer contracts with the landlord for the holding to be placed in a certain condition of repair; also that the tenant shall provide certain fixtures, or movable furniture, tools, cattle, etc.

The Irish landlord is not obligated to provide anything except the bare soil, not even houses or barns, fences or drainage. Buildings, fixtures, tools and cattle must be provided by the tenant. They are his property while he remains. But if he leaves a holding he receives no compensation for any buildings he may erect or any repairs he may make. This is a most fruitful source and cause of dissatisfaction and turmoil among tenants.

ARTICLE VII.

THE AGRICULTURAL CONDITION OF THE ISLAND.
[Continued.]

Another fruitful source of irritation lies in the fact that not only is the Irish peasant forced to make all the improvements upon his holding, but also the landlord has the power to increase the rent, on account of the increased value which the tenant has given to the land through his own outlay of labor and money. In many cases where the tenant has reclaimed bog land, the rent . has soon been raised to several times the value in fee simple of the land before the tenant had reclaimed it. The fact that all improvements, all fences, houses and even ditches and drains are made by the tenant is used to support the claim that the tenant has, in justice and equity, a certain proprietary right in the soil which he has contributed so much to improve in condition and value.

The above does not apply to any large extent to the mode of leasing the estates in the Ulster provinces in the north of Ireland. There the so-called "Tenant Right" system prevails. By this is meant that the tenant has the ownership in the improvements he has made, and that, when a change in tenants is made, for any reason, the new tenant is compelled to purchase, at a fair valuation, all the improvements which his predecessor has made on the holding. It will be noticed, however, that under the "Tenant Right" system, the landlord does not pay for nor purchase the improvements which any succession of tenants may make on his land.

It is urged by some that the extension of the Ulster "Tenant Right" system to the middle and southern parts of Ireland would cure the land troubles of the island. Indeed, this system was legalized for the whole island in 1870, but it is practically carried into effect but little beyond the province of Ulster. It is charged that the advantages of this system are greatly neutralized by the right of the landlords to advance the rent at will.

The soil of Ireland is of very unequal quality and excellence. It is one of the most unfortunate circumstances in the land question, that in the parts of Ireland containing the poorest soil there is the greatest proportion of very small holdings. In Connaught, for example, many hundreds, if not thousands, of families eke out a miserable existence from holdings containing only from half an acre to an acre, and this of most wretched soil. These miserable tenants, who have no practical knowledge beyond the rudest processes of agriculture, are only able to keep their families from starvation by the addition to their income of cash which they derive from going to England and working for farmers there during the harvest season.

The utter failure of crops in England in 1879 cut off this addition to the income of the poverty-stricken Irish tenant farmers. The introduction into England of the modern American system of gathering harvests by machinery threatens to cut off permanently this aid to Irish farmers, even when the crops are excellent in quality and quantity.

It will be easily imagined that under all these untoward circumstances the great improvements which during the last thirty years have entirely revolutionized the science of agriculture, and which have added so greatly to the wealth of farms and farmers in advanced countries of Europe and America, have been adopted by only a very small proportion of the farmers in Ireland. As a rule the mode of cultivating the soil is exceedingly rude and primitive. In many parts the plough is unknown, and the spade and the hoe are the only utensils employed. Through lack of means, enterprise and knowledge, fertilizers are rarely used. The mild and moist atmosphere furnishes the chief nourishment to the potato, which is the staple and often the sole vegetable grown on the acre or the half acre held by the wretched tenant. A slight addition to the moisture of the weather during the late summer or the early fall causes this single crop of potatoes to rot before they ripen, and thus famine and starvation stare several millions of these wretched "farmers" in the face.

The original division of the population into tribes (or clans) prevailed in Ireland, as in Scotland, until the close of the seventeenth century, or until the suppression of the Rebellion by Cromwell, that is, nearly a thousand years after it had been abolished in England and France. The influence of this tribal system has been one of the chief causes of the present subdivision of large estates into exceedingly small holdings. Indeed, in many regards, Ireland is a *primitive country*, as much so as Albania, Turkestan or Senegambia. Some astute English sociologists even claim that this primitive condition of society is an advantage to the British Empire, since it furnishes a source to supply the race exhaustion, which history has shown to befall every nation, sooner or later, that does not renew its vigor from some primitive stock of people. This fact of the primitive state of a large part of the population of Ireland, and their backwardness in entering the tide of civilization, which has flowed so steadily forward in England and the continent of Europe for the last thousand years, is a most important element in understanding the troubles which are continually agitating this island. The condition would be in a certain measure repeated, if the State of Georgia or Alabama were settled wholly by blacks, who were portioned out upon parcels of land of from half an acre to five or ten acres to a family, the blacks being left to cultivate the land in any way they might choose, but being compelled to pay heavy rents to white landlords, residing at a distance, with whom the black tenants never come into personal communication, relationship or friendship.

As a combined result of all the historical influences which we have traced at some length in previous articles, of the primitive condition of the large portion of the Irish population, and of the extreme poverty of the miserable tenants of small holdings, we can easily see what is the moral status of the people. Here, as elsewhere, the old proverb holds good, that Satan finds occupation for idle hands. The lower the grade of civilization, the more base and groveling the forms of vice which idleness induces. The coarse drunkenness and brawling which are found constantly in the villages of Ireland make that country a by-word among the nations of Europe. The general morality of the people is of the lowest possible grade.

Enforced idleness has entailed upon an important portion of the population habits of indolence, unthriftiness and uncleanness, out of which they cannot be lifted without external help. The extreme degradation of the population of southern and western Ireland has attracted the attention of writers and travelers for centuries. After the close of the Rebellion which Cromwell crushed, Sir W. Petty writes : "These 1,100,000 people do live in about 200,000 families or houses, whereof there are about 16,000 which have more than one chimney in each, and about 24,000 which have but one; all the other houses, being 160,000, are wretched, nasty cabins without chimney, window or door-shut, even worse than those of the savage American Indians."

In 1835 a French political economist, Gustave de Beaumont, visited Ireland. He writes: " I have seen the Indian in his forests and the negro in his chains, and I thought I had beheld the lowest term of human misery; but I did not then know the lot of Ireland. Irish misery forms a type by itself, of which there exists nowhere else either model or imitation. In seeing it one recognizes that no theoretical limits can be assigned to the misfortunes of nations. The condition which in Ireland is above poverty would be among other people frightful distress. The miserable classes which in France are justly pitied would form in Ireland a privileged class." The German historian Von Raumer, writing in the same year, says: " No words could express the frightful truth which in Ireland everywhere meets the eye." The distinguished German traveler Kohl. says : " The Tartars of the Crimea are poor and barbarous, but they look at least like human beings; but nowhere save in Ireland can be found human creatures living from one year's end to another on the same root, berry or weed. There are animals, indeed, that live so, but human beings nowhere, save in Ireland." In the same year the English traveler Inglis writes: " It is undeniable that the condition of the Irish poor is immeasurably worse than that of the West India slave." Barrow writes : " No picture drawn by the pencil, none by the pen, can possibly convey an idea of the sad reality. There is no other country on the face of the earth in which such extreme misery prevails as in Ireland." The Abbe Perraud wrote in 1860 : " How great was my astonishment, twenty years after the journey of Beaumont, to come upon the very same destitution which he so eloquently described in 1835 ! The lot of the poorest peasant in France cannot compare with the misery of a large part of Ireland." All careful and observing travelers have noticed the same terrible destitution and misery, even when there is no special failure of crops and consequent famine.

We have spoken thus far only of the misery of the tenants of the smaller holdings. The present agitation in Ireland is only on behalf of the *tenant farmers.* But there is another class, whose misery is lower, if possible, than that of this smaller class of tenants. That is the class of *floating laborers,* who have no fixed home, but depend upon the tenant farmers for employment. There are 600,000 tenants, whose families include over 3,000,000 people, or rather more than half the entire population. There are, perhaps, 250,000 people engaged in trades and manufactures, representing a population of about 1,000,000. There remain, perhaps, 600,000 floating laborers. One-half of these are employed on the large farms at a little above starvation wages. The remainder, representing a population of about 1,000,000, are the most forlorn and wretched people of this most wretched island. They are every year and almost every month upon the verge of starvation.

A few further important points remain to be considered, in order to gain a comprehensive and intelligent idea of the influences which intensify the destitution and sufferings of Ireland.

Perhaps, first of all, should be mentioned the "absenteeism" of most of the landlords. Large estates in Ireland are owned by corporations in England. The incomes from this class of estates are sent to England and do not return to enrich, in any form, the country from which they are drawn. Many of the owners of large estates, obtaining them frequently by inheritance, never go to Ireland at all, but receive their rents through the medium of "middle-men," or agents. Some landlords occasionally visit their estates and, during their short residence there, hold that sort of diminutive "court," which the British, like other aristocracies, hold at the mansions or castles where they temporarily or permanently reside. The complaint against "absentee" landlords is that the income from their estates is taken out of Ireland and is spent in England, thus constantly and permanently draining Ireland of a portion of her wealth. But it is said that the wealthy landlord finds little congenial society in Ireland; the prospect of being shot at by some shiftless but embittered and revengeful cottier does not add to the attractiveness, to a landlord and his family, of a residence in Ireland. On the other hand the great British capital, London, the seaside resorts of Great Britain, and the genial climate, social advantages and art treasures of the Continent, offer positive advantages for residence to the landlords and their families. Besides, many owners of estates in Ireland own also estates in England and Scotland, on which they prefer to reside. With all this, the two great evils complained of concerning "absenteeism" are that the income from the estates is not spent in the country, and that the owners of the land have no personal oversight of tenants and little sympathy with their sufferings.

Another evil, which is the outgrowth of absenteeism, lies in the fact that the landlords often employ " middle-men," or agents, to arrange the holdings, and to fix and collect the rents. It is to the interest of middle-men to keep the rents up as high as possible, and to pursue with relentless vigor tenants who are backward in their payment of rent.

Another drain upon the resources of Ireland consists in the Imperial taxes, which are taken from this country and expended in the conduct of the civil government and the military and naval establishments in England. Through Imperial taxation some £5,000,000 is drained from Ireland every year.

The exportations of food, grain and hay from Ireland to England amount to about £60,000,000 every year. There is thus seen the apparently anomalous spectacle of vast quantities of provisions being sent away to a distant market, from districts where a large portion of the population are upon the verge of starvation. It has been exceedingly difficult to get down to the ultimate facts as to the real amount of unusual distress in certain seasons, from the fact that after relief committees have distributed charity through certain regions, tenants and laborers, who have accepted relief, have been known to send to market, from a hidden pit, large quantities of potatoes. This dishonesty and duplicity has led many Englishmen to hear with doubt and incredulity the oft-repeated cries of distress from this ever-discussed but little-understood Ireland. The exportation of food must follow the laws of trade, during times of famine as well as at other times. There is no reason why a farmer who has a thousand bushels of potatoes to sell should not send them to the best market, be it Liverpool or Glasgow, and take the money to pay his rent and his laborers. Nor should he feel personally bound to divide his potatoes with his poor or starving countrymen ten miles distant. Still the startling and horrible fact often occurs that destitute and starving people see wagons laden with potatoes pass by their very doors, under police escort, to the steamer dock, to be borne away to hated England. What wonder that tumults and riots thus occur !

ARTICLE VIII.

FEASIBLE AND UNFEASIBLE REMEDIES FOR THE LAND TROUBLES.

The gravity of the sufferings and distress of the agricultural population of Ireland has attracted the active attention of statesmen, political economists and philanthropists in England for the last fifty years. Statesmen from the continent of Europe have made careful studies of the extraordinary and phenomenal economic condition of this country, as the German Von Raumer, the French De Beaumont, and the Italian Sismondi and Cavour. During the past two years British newspapers, magazines and reviews have been flooded with articles treating of the subject from every standpoint. Every possible project for curing these evils which the human imagination could conjure up has been devised and presented. The most radical of these, perhaps, is the heroic proposition of a cold-blooded conservative to "sink the island fifty feet below the level of the ocean for forty-eight hours, and then to lift it up and commence anew !" On the other extreme, the most radical but equally impracticable communistic and socialistic schemes have had open champions. Of serious schemes, which have had strong, earnest and combined advocates, we shall present a few of the most prominent and important.

First of all we may mention the scheme of the "Land Leaguers," under the leadership of Mr. Parnell. The Land League is a secret organization, and only a portion of its plans and principles have been made public. One of the announced principles is to have all tenants agree to pay only a certain rental, which is to be a certain percentage upon the valuation of the land as assessed in 1841, called the "Griffith's Valuation," from the name of the superintendent of the census at that time. To enforce this, they agree to hold no communication, by way of trade, with any tenant who pays any higher rate of rent, with any landlord who evicts tenants for non-payment of rent, with any farmer who takes a holding from which a tenant has been evicted, or with any tradesman who buys or sells of such a tenant or landlord.   This feature of the Land League movement is an invasion upon the laws of property as recognized in all civilized lands.   The League also proposes, by continued agitation, within legal and constitutional limits, to bring about a change in the mode of tenure of land in Ireland.   It is barely possible, though not probable, that this agitation may lead to legislation by Parliament which will alleviate in some degree the causes of distress in Ireland.   But it has within itself no elements of success in the main object for which it has been organized.

Another project goes by the name of " Home Rule," by which is meant the dissolving of the Imperial Parliament, and the re-establishment of the Irish Parliament.   This would involve a large additional expense to Ireland.   The new Parliament would be under the control of the landlords.   Or, if a contest should arise between landlords and tenants, it would probably end in turmoil and riot.   But the probability of Home Rule being conceded by the Imperial Parliament is too small to be seriously considered.

A few extremists claim that the balm for Ireland's woes is to be found in perfect national independence—in entire separation from the British Crown.   This, if attainable at all, could only be reached through a long and bloody struggle, which would add immeasurably to the immediate and future woes of Ireland.   It is difficult to see how, even if national independence were peaceably granted to-morrow, the social, political and economical elements, as they exist to-day, could be molded into a harmonious, or, indeed, into an endurable state of social order; or how the sufferings of the small holders and of the floating laborers could be thereby in any regard relieved or removed.   Like Home Rule, Irish independence will not be granted.

Another project which has been favorably advocated by many philanthropic statesmen, both British and continental, is the establishment of an extensive system of " Peasant Proprietorship." By this is meant the cutting up of many or all of the large estates into small farms, which shall become the property of the class who are now tenant farmers. Thus the cultivators of the soil will become the owners, and will have an interest in it, which, as tenants, they never can have. Many plans have been suggested for effectuating this scheme. Some have proposed that the Imperial Government shall buy up all the estates in Ireland, and shall then divide the land anew into holdings of about thirty acres each. These holdings, or farms, are to be sold to the present tenant farmers on long time. Thirty-five years, or the average length of a generation, has been proposed as the time of payment, which is to be made in equal annual installments.

It is charged by opponents to this scheme that it is utterly visionary; and that, even if possible, it would only add greatly to the disasters of Ireland. Thus, the hundreds of millions of pounds of purchase money would be taken from Ireland by the present owners, be they landlords or London corporations, and would be invested in England. Also the annual payments by the farmers would be transferred to the bank of England, in London, and would be a constant and disastrous drain upon the wealth of Ireland, and thus would lead to its further and more ruinous impoverishment. And if the peasants are unable to pay rent, how much more would it be impossible for them to make the payments on the principal purchase money which will necessarily be greater than the rent. It is further urged that in less than a generation the laws of thriftiness and unthriftiness will prevail here as elsewhere, and thus large estates will eventually be formed out of these smaller ones. And, on the other hand, since the law of primogeniture is to be abolished, as these thirty acre farms are divided among children, in one or two generations the present condition of exceedingly small farms will be repeated, with the necessary accompaniment of misery and starvation. Further, the large present class of very small farmers and the large body of floating laborers, which include the chief portion of the destitute poor, are lacking in that knowledge of modern farming and in those thrifty habits which are indispensable for success in the management of farms of larger size. Thus the beautiful scheme of dividing Ireland up among a large class of "Peasant Proprietors" is utopian in the extreme; it would increase, instead of diminishing the present poverty and suffering ; it would bring only temporary not permanent relief ; and there is not the . slightest probability that it will ever be attempted.

Another equally visionary half-measure which has been proposed is to transfer the tenants of excessively small holdings, in regions where the soil is very poor, to other regions where the soil is rich and productive. Upon this and other impracticable schemes it is easy to do a deal of fine talking and writing. During the weary years of our late war, how easy it was for brilliant Bohemians, sitting cosily in their sanctums, to criticise the generals in the field, and map out campaigns which would terminate the struggle in three months ! The proposition to transfer population from one region of Ireland to another involves the violation of all rights of property and of individual liberty. It might be done in an Asiatic despotism, but it cannot be done in Ireland, under Anglo-Saxon rule.

There is one feasible means of relieving the poverty and destitution in Ireland. In our opinion this is the sole practicable mode of relief. That is the *emigration of the surplus population.* But for the emigration of the past fifty years, the population of that island to-day would be fifteen or twenty, instead of five or six millions. Famine and starvation, instead of returning at intervals, would be the overwhelming chronic and constant condition of the island. Emigration is the legitimate and natural safety-valve for the escape of surplus population in all civilized countries. This is particularly the case at the present time, owing to the extraordinary development of means of communication during the last twenty, and especially the last ten years. It is easier for the Irish peasant to go from Cork or Dublin to Manitoba or Texas to-day, than it was for our pioneers to go from New York or Boston to Syracuse or Rochester sixty years ago. The vast and rich but uncultivated fields of Minnesota, Manitoba and Texas invite the starving or straitened, the thrifty and enterprising tillers of the soil of all lands to go thither and find food, abundance and wealth.

The government of the " British Dominion" in North America has made most liberal offers of land, and of aid in transportation, to the suffering and destitute people of Ireland. Indeed every

Irish man or woman who arrives in New York, though possessed
of no trade or skill in labor, if willing to work is sure of employment at wages which will more than keep soul and body
together.   In a few months, or, at most, in a few years, they can
earn enough to send for brothers and sisters to escape from the
land of desolation to a land of plenty.

Every prosperous Irishman in America, Canada or Australia;
every Irish servant girl, living in the midst of bounty in our kitch-
ens; every immigrant from any of the over-populated countries of
Europe, is a living argument for emigration, not as a palliative,
but as a radical cure of the evils and miseries which inevitably
accompany a too compact population in a given territory.

We are not to lose sight of the fact that Ireland is essentially
an agricultural country.   No legislation as to the tenure of land
can make it a manufacturing country like Belgium, or a commercial country like Holland.   Its rural population is, also, the most
dense in the known world.   The only escape for this excessively
compact rural population from misery and starvation will be in
the future, as it has been in the past, through emigration to such
countries as America, where vast regions of most fertile virgin
soil have for endless ages been awaiting the approach of civilized
man.

It is not too much to say that a people who, with their
opportunities of escape, persist in sitting down and hugging their
misery, in living in rags, dirty hovels and mire, more like the
swine with whom they lodge than like human beings, thereby cut
themselves off from the intelligent sympathy of the world.   The
only palliating circumstances are the ignorance, the stupidity and
inherited inertia which cloud the vision, obscure the judgment
and dull the senses of the poorest portion of the Irish peasants,
who are, indeed, in a "primitive condition of society."

But, for the more intelligent and somewhat well-to-do class
of tenant farmers, while in sight and hearing of the fleets
of steamers which every week pass from Liverpool to the south,
and from Glasgow to the north of Ireland, on their way to America,—for these larger farmers to sluggishly stay and contest with
the difficulties of their surroundings, and then to send Mr.
Parnell to America to secure funds to help their Land League

agitations, is a great strain upon the patience of intelligent Americans: For Mr. Parnell himself and his coadjutors (or co-conspirators) to make political capital out of the miseries of the Irish farmer and laborer is for him to invite the contempt of every well-informed philanthropist, political economist or statesman. It is safe to predict that within less than a twelvemonth Mr. Parnell and his associates will sink into as despised or ludicrous oblivion as have the Fenian heroes who, a few years ago, held high court on Union Square and organized a Quixotic raid into Canada.

It is a curious circumstance that the majority of writers and statesmen belonging to the conservative party in England, together with many liberals of all shades, favor emigration as the only natural and feasible relief of the Irish at home. The conservatives may find an additional argument from the fact that this mode does not disturb the question of tenure of landed or other property in England. It is, indeed, an instructive circumstance, and a just occasion for alarm, as to its bearing upon the tenure of all property, of all kinds, and in all countries, that Mr. Parnell goes to Paris and holds confidential communication with Rochefort, Victor Hugo and other pronounced Communists, Socialists and Nihilists.

It will without doubt be true in the future, as it has been in the past, that the more enterprising of the poorer classes will emigrate from Ireland, leaving, the more stupid and shiftless at home, there to continue the most prolific propagation of the proletariat that is to be found in any part of the world. But no impediment on this account ought to be put, nor has ever been put, by the British Government in the way of the emigration of the thriftier portion of the poorer classes from Ireland, whether their destination be England, Canada, the United States or Australia.

In conclusion, we are not to lose sight of the fact that causes entirely external to Ireland are conspiring to render this island incapable of supporting even one-half of its present population. The chief of these is the development and rapid expansion of what is termed in Europe the " American" system of farming. The first contest of the *Monitor* with the *Merrimac* sent to the bottom of the ocean all the wooden vessels of war in the world. Mr. Dalrymple's farm in Minnesota has sounded the death-knell of all old-fashioned farming. Profitable farming to-day, whether in Minnesota, Ohio, England or Ireland, means the substitution of machinery for human hands, of a reaping machine drawn by two horses for a hundred men with sickles. The partial introduction of the machine system of farming into England has already cut off a part of the demand for Irish laborers in England during the harvest season. When modern farming is fully adopted in Ireland, as of necessity will soon be the case, it will be found that three-quarters of the present number of farm laborers will be put out of employment. A population of one million will furnish laborers sufficient to conduct all the farming operations. Another million, more or less, will live by manufactures and trade. The remainder will have to emigrate or starve, irrespective of Tenant Right, Peasant Proprietorship, Free Sale, Fixity of Tenure, Fair Rents, or any other condition of ownership, tenantry or labor !

The effects of machine farming, as practiced upon the vast prairies of our Western States, are already felt in every country in Europe. American wheat, cheese, beef and fruit are already disturbing the local markets, and therefore the prosperity of the farming population in France, Germany, Italy, Spain, and even Russia. The advance of civilization brings with it, from time to time, economic changes of vast extent. It is an irreparable law that the old must adapt itself to the new. The transition in modes of farming operations in different countries in Europe will be necessarily attended by financial disturbance and, in many cases, doubtless, by great distress. The chief relief will be found in emigration of the farming population to countries where are found vast regions of fertile and unoccupied land. While ease, competence and affluence await those who have the energy to lift themselves from the surroundings and attachments of home and country and go to distant lands and foreign climes, we may pity but cannot approve the lassitude and inertia of those who prefer to remain in distress and wretchedness, meanwhile proclaiming their misery to the ends of the earth.

APPENDIX.

MR. GLADSTONE'S NEW LAND BILL.

After the foregoing pages were put to press, Mr. Gladstone's Land Bill was introduced in the House of Commons and passed its first reading. Parliament has just adjourned for the Easter recess amid great excitement, and the bill has been re-committed, after having received twenty-one amendments in the House of Commons. This bill is spoken of by the English papers as by far the most important which the present Premier has ever framed. Its most important feature is the following: it proposes to establish a system of local commissions or courts, to which shall be referred all questions of dispute as to rents, which may arise between landlords and tenants. The decisions of these courts are to be final.

This bill is regarded by all conservatives and many liberals as revolutionary; as destructive of rights of property, according to the British constitution and the usages in all civilized countries and in all ages of the world; and, finally, as communistic in its spirit and results. The Duke of Argyle has resigned his place in the Gladstone Cabinet, since he sympathizes with this view concerning the bill. During the recess the members of Parliament will have an opportunity of conferring with their constituents and ascertaining the general public opinion with reference to the bill.

Meantime the telegraph brings report of great excitement extending through southern and western Ireland, growing out of an attack upon a constabulary force who were attending a bailiff who was serving a writ of ejectment. A riotous uprising is feared throughout Ireland.

It is also stated that thousands of young Irishmen and Irishwomen, of good appearance and apparently of some means, are crowding the steamers at Dublin and Cork, in their rage to emigrate to Canada and the United States.